Basics for New Dog Owners

Table of Contents:

1. Understanding ingredients
2. Dogs need different diets at different ages
3. Vitamin and mineral supplements
4. Boredom and variety
5. Cost of feeds
6. Dry vs. Canned food
7. Home made diets
8. Food allergies
9. How much should I feed my dog?
10. How often should I feed my dog?
11. Signs of Ill health
12. Heart worm, fleas and other parasites
13. Heart worm prevention
14. Common questions about heart worm
15. Fleas and other parasites
16. Do parasites cause "Scooting"?
17. Preventing dental disease
18. Home dental care
19. Veterinary dental treatments
20. The importance of the physical examination
21. Why are regular check-ups important?
22. What happens during an examination?
23. How often should my pet be examined?
24. How to administer medicine
25. Nursing a sick dog
26. Vaccinations
27. Common questions about vaccinations
28. Spaying and neutering
29. Spaying of the Female dog
30. Surgical neutering of the male dog
31. Pet health insurance
32. Clipping a dog
33. First steps in grooming

34. Bathing a dog
35. Pet Identification

LEGAL NOTICE:

The Publisher has strived to be as accurate and complete as possible in the creation of this report, notwithstanding the fact that he does not warrant or represent at any time that the contents within are accurate due to the rapidly changing nature of the Internet.

While all attempts have been made to verify information provided in this publication, the Publisher assumes no responsibility for errors, omissions, or contrary interpretation of the subject matter herein. Any perceived slights of specific persons, peoples, or organizations are unintentional.

This book is a common sense guide to dog owner basics. In practical advice books, like anything else in life, there are no guarantees of any kind made. Readers are cautioned to reply on their own judgment about their individual circumstances to act accordingly.

This book is not intended for use as a source of basics of dog ownership. All readers are advised to seek services of competent professionals in the perspective fields.

You are encouraged to print this book for easy reading.

1. Understanding ingredients

Understanding the ingredients of your dog's food items is a must for the dog lovers or dog owners. Whenever you feed the dog with different kinds of food items, you should always read the label and understand the contents about the dog feed types that are being used in such commercial preparations. You should understand the ingredients while buying food for your dog and also know what to look for.

Feed items include dry and fresh food. The fresh dog food that is prepared in homes generally consists of ingredients like freshly cut chicken pieces in addition to the cranberry juices, blue-green algae, etc.

If you come across any different kinds of preservatives and if the dog develops all of a sudden signs pertaining to the food allergy, suspect the unwanted ingredient in the feed items given. Similarly, understand about the moisture status. If the food item is having more moisture, then the dog may prefer this as well.

Beet pulp, pasta, Soy bean oil, wheat middlings, calcium carbonate, magnesium oxide, copper sulphate, iron sulphate, zinc oxide, choline chloride, etc. are often the ingredients in case of vegetarian based diet items offered to the pet animals like dogs.

Raw egg, chicken, beef, mutton, fish, quail etc. are often the preferred ingredients in case of dog diets that are prepared on the basis of the non-vegetarian items. Taurine is one of the essential ingredients for the dog's nutrition. Like wise, in the case of dogs feed with frozen fish items, the vitamin called thiamine needs to be supplemented as an ingredient.

Many premium type of dog food preparations contain essential fatty acids, carbohydrates with adequate fiber contents, vitamins like A, D, E and B complex vitamins.

Furthermore, minerals like zinc, is an essential ingredient for skin health status and calcium, which is an essential ingredient for bone growth, tonicity of muscles. They should be enriched in these food items. However, the cost of those food preparations are comparatively more expensive than the food preparations with general ingredients. Though it may be better for your dog's health.

2. Dogs need different diets at different ages

Dogs need different diets at different ages. Yes. This is true. For example, the puppy needs milk as the major food item while an adult dog may need beef or chicken in addition to the boiled egg and milk. So depending on the age factor, the diet schedule varies in reality for the dogs like any other species.

Puppies need greater amounts of protein, fat and carbohydrates than an adult dogs. Furthermore, puppies need more frequent feeding schedules in a day, unlike an adult dog. The movement based requirements of diet are more in the case of puppies, since they are often more active than the adult dogs.

Elder dogs need restricted protein but the protein needs to be easily digestible and easily assimilated in the body. The diet schedule should have ample supply of water for them. Feeding aged dogs too much protein may finally lead to over burden to the renal structures and ultimately, the dog may end up damaging filters in the kidney.

This is true especially when the immune system of these dogs is compromised due to many factors. Similarly, the elderly dogs need less food only because the movements of the adult dogs are highly restricted and hence, they have to spend a limited of energy.

Female dogs in the pregnancy stage need not be fed a full stomach since it may cause some discomforts to the animal. However, the pregnant animal and the nursing animal need special type of food items that deliver a balanced type of nutrition with proper supplementation of vitamins and minerals.

The nursing animal with puppies need to be fed with enough amounts of calcium and hence, there will not be any calcium based deficiency and the bones of the puppies will be strong without any curving.

3. Vitamin and mineral supplements

Vitamin and mineral supplements are the most important components in any dog's feeding. If there is a balance in the vitamin and mineral supplements, then the animal will have a healthy life and hence, the immunity is not compromised in an unwanted way. This simply means that there the dog will be more disease resistance against various diseases.

Pet owners should know that vitamins A, D, E, and K are the fat-soluble vitamins and others are water-soluble vitamins. Vitamins like thiamine, pyridoxine and cyanocobalamin are important for the functions of nervous system. Deficiency of vitamin A leads to night blindness and skin lesions and deficiency of vitamin D leads to the softening and weakening of the bones.

These problems are many a time encountered by the dog owners. Among these, vitamin A toxicities may occur if you feed them in excessive amounts, like vitamin D. Hence, give emphasis on this while you are using these vitamins in the dogs. Cod liver oil from selected fishes has more vitamin A in them and are universally good feed for dogs.

All dogs may not need supplements of minerals or vitamins to live well for the moment, but it is important for their future. If they become sick or aged or very young without proper feeding, supplementations are required for the upkeep of health status in them. However, one has to follow the instructions of veterinarian in this regard.

If the dogs are fed with fish in frozen conditions, then they may be suffering constantly from vitamin B1 deficiency and hence, such dogs need to be given specifically B1. Careless supplementations of minerals may lead to diseases and hence, veterinarians always need to be consulted on the supplementation of minerals or vitamins.

Minerals like calcium, magnesium, zinc, manganese, iron, copper etc. are given more emphasis in addition to sodium and potassium. Zinc is related to skin health and potassium is related to the muscle health and calcium with phosphorus is related to the bone health.

However, if you feed the dog with chicken, mutton or beef along with required vegetables, artificial supplementation of mineral or vitamin tablets may be highly reduced but supplements need to be thought of when you are not able to maintain a balanced nutrition as this happens with most of the dogs, due to multifaceted causes.

4. Boredom and variety

Boredom and variety are always inter connected in case of dog misbehaving. Yes. This is true. Many a times, boredom can be managed with variety of materials that will distract the animals to a greater extent. Hence, the dog may not do the abnormal or unwanted activity arising out of the boredom experienced by it.

Boredom experienced dogs may have different types of behavioral patterns. For example, some dogs will be seen barking continuously and some may be engaged always in some digging activities.

There are many ways to get your dog out of its boredom activities. Many toys are available which simulated duck, dog, rodent etc.

These may be kept inside the crate and in particular, puppies love these items. A buster cube with multiple treats may be placed in the dog's shelter and the animal soon understands on how to roll the buster cube to get the treats it prefers. A Buster Cube is an ingenious toy use for simulating and activating your dog during play and feed time. Instead of placing the food monotonously in one place, change the place of feeding suddenly.

Such actions will be helpful for removing the boredom like activity in your dog. Activities pertaining to boredom need to be redefined well by the dog owners. This will help them to a greater extent to drive away the unwanted behavior patterns in their pet dogs.

For example, some dogs may often have destructive biting characters and will be seen biting chair, cloth, mats, and everything that can see. After ruling out the teething problem if it is a puppy, provide it with some large sized balls, mineral mixture based bone materials, etc. Such variety of materials help to reduce the boredom related activities.

5. Cost of feeds

The cost of dog feed is one factor that is most important in the case of feeding of dogs with different kinds of food items. Yes. This is true. The cost factor needs to be looked into in various perspectives during the preparation of the food items, required for the balanced feeding of dogs with proper vitamin and mineral supplementations in the food.

Cost will not always matter much because the dog's value is being assessed in terms of companionship and the happiness derived from the dog to the dog owner. Though the cost of the food items is comparatively more, many dog owners don't mind much due to the increased benefits derived from their dogs in terms of protection, guiding, etc.

Selection of ingredients for the home made food needs to be however based on the quality factor. Even when the quality is more, general persons may seek some cheaper items only. Recommended nutrient contents may be obtained from the national nutrient academies in all nations and this will provide guidelines.

One can correlate the cost factor with items available in their own country. Generally, the commercial food items are expensive especially the ones that use the modern technologies of food preparation like oven-baking, sterilization of cans, air drying or freeze drying of contents etc.

Canned items cost more than the dry food items. However, the cost of the items depends on what kind of food item to be used for the dogs. Food allergies need to be monitored during usage of different food items in case of dogs due to the cheaper cost of the items. Often the quality need not be compromised because of the cost factor.

Most of the dog food items nowadays have mentioned their cost in the label itself. Hence, the dog owner need not have any problem in taking a decision on the purchase.

6. Dry vs. Canned food

These types of food materials are different with different grades of liking by the dogs. Dogs like dry foods only if they are tasty only and however, on comparison, the dogs prefer only the canned food items. Reason for such preference by the dogs is that in case of canned food items, the moisture is about seventy to eighty per cent but in case of dry food, it is only about ten per cent.

However, if you view it in terms of nutrients, often the dry food contains nearly ninety per cent nutrients whereas the canned food items contain only less per cent of nutrients and most of the times. It is only soy products that are structured so well to look like meat pieces.

Hence, to make up the nutritional balance in the body systems, the dog has to eat more amounts of canned food materials than the dry food materials. Hence, just compare the cost factor related to this feature by you. Many dry food items are soybean and rice based.

Now some dry food items are based on corn. Sometimes, beef based or chicken based food items come in the cans along with mineral and vitamin supplements suited for the upkeep of the dog's health status. Larger dogs that weigh more than thirty pounds need to be fed with semi moist food items or dry food items in most of the occasions.

This is to satisfy the food receptors in the stomach. This is due to the fact that the larger dogs need to eat plenty of moist food or the canned food items to satisfy these criteria. But it may not be practically possible in these larger dogs. The small sized dogs may have a satisfactory level of nutrients if fed even the moist food items. However, the caloric density of the dry food should not be forgotten. Enriched dry food items are highly welcome ones than the non - enriched food items.

7. Home made diets

Home made diets are important in the dog feeding. Many a times, the commercial diets consist of food items that have artificial coloring agents and flavoring agents that are harmful to the dog's body. Home made food items have the guarantee of freshness in the preparation unlike the ready-made commercial items.

The preservatives added in the commercial food items may not be the suitable ones to the dogs from the health point of view. Even in case of renal diseases in dogs, the home made diets may be made with ground beef, slices of bread, calcium carbonate, boiled eggs etc.

The purpose is to have the restricted protein supply in the feed items prepared. This should be carried out with home made diets prepared exclusively for the dogs suffering from renal diseases. Water is added in sufficient quantities to help the proper metabolism in the digestion-impaired renal cases.

The dog may have allergic symptoms like severe itching, which may not get corrected by different kinds of medications employed over a period of time. Such cases may get easily treated once the dog food is changed from the commercial type of food to the home made food items.

Often, the home made food items are prepared using the freezing procedures to kill the germs or by adding grape seed extracts to provide sufficient antioxidants to the home made food items. Food grade vinegar is also added in many times to the meat pieces prepared in a fresh manner. All these can be enriched with vitamin supplements that are available in fruit essences, fish oil etc.

Cranberry juice, bananas, fish and meat are prepared in a quality manner and no preservatives are added during the preparation of these kinds of food items and the dog becomes more active after the consumption of such food items.

8. Food allergies

Food allergies are something that is difficult to identify unless one is well aware of the baseline information with regard to this type of allergy. The main symptoms of food allergies in dogs include the facial itching, limb chewing, belly itching, recurrent ear infections or skin infections.

Since the dogs consume lot of prepared food materials including various kinds of proteins, fillers, coloring agents and more; in the commercial food materials, the incidences of food allergies are more than one can imagine. Allergic reactions mostly involve the skin or the gastro intestinal tract.

If you come across your dog itching after the provision of specific food materials, then suspect the food allergy in this animal. However, conditions like fungal infections need to be ruled out in general before the conclusion of itching as a sign of food allergy.

There are many recorded incidences of allergies of dogs to corn or to wheat. However, the food allergies vary from dog to dog. Read the labels clearly before feeding your dogs with pet food materials, in such occasions. Too much colored food materials may be avoided since they may cause allergies to your dog.

Food allergies are often linked to the hyper active behavior noticed in the dogs. Added colors, preservatives, and high fat diet might cause such food allergies in the dogs and hence, one has to be careful in providing new kind of diet to their dogs and closely monitor the dog for any signs of allergy.

There are many occasions that food allergies might be diagnosed in the dogs but the dog may have other problems like pancreatitis. To rule out the food allergies, observation your dogs everytime you feed them, look for reasons to link the signs of dog with food given, specific signs encountered, differential diagnosis etc. are the important features to be given emphasis.

9. How much should I feed my dog?

Many people will give different types of answers based on their experience with their dogs. However, the scientific facts related to the feeding aspects in case of dogs need to be given emphasis during the feeding activities maintained in case of dogs.

Usually the puppies should not be separated before they are eight weeks old. However, some times the orphaned puppies may exist. Usually about five percent of the body weight may be taken as criteria for the quantity of food to be given to the puppies. However, the amount that is consumed by the dog varies with size of the dogs also.

However, one can have a thumb rule of feeding the puppy goes until you see visible fullness of the abdomen to a moderate degree. If you are going on feeding the animal without giving emphasis to the animal's stomach appearance, then the puppy may experience some kinds of digestive upsets and the diarrhea may occur in them.

This may cause many inconveniences to the owner as well as the puppy. Unlike adult dogs, the puppies need to be fed with restricted amounts of food but in more frequencies. However, once the age advances, the amount may be increased to some extent but the frequency of feeding is often decreased in many occasions.

A dog on a raw diet may consume only two to four percent of their body weight. Just observe closely the feeding pattern of the dog and the body condition of the animal. If the dog becomes obese, just reduce the quantity of food and if the dog becomes thin, then have an increase in the feeding items.

As mentioned earlier, puppies and adolescent dogs eat more than the adult dogs. Likewise the geriatric dog eats less than the adult dog due to the reduced movements of the dog. However, remember to restrict the amounts of protein during the feeding of diet to the aged dogs.

10. How often should I feed my dog?

This often becomes an important question asked by many dog lovers and dog owners. If it is a puppy within age of the first six weeks, the puppies need to be given milk at the rate of five to seven times per day. The puppy will make some sound if it wants to feed in general.

However, the feeding frequency may be reduced when the dog becomes six to eight weeks old. By the time the dog assumes the age of four weeks, it may start taking of some solid food. Hence, mix the solid food with water in majority and feed your puppy once or twice in the beginning and if the dog develops some diarrhea, then delay the feeding.

Most of the times, it is due to trial and error but taking some basic steps in feeding, so you need to watch out. The feeding frequency may be changed to two to three times after the assumption of age of eight weeks. However, if the dog is seen hungry craving for food, then provide food once than the estimated numbers. This varies with different breeds of dogs.

However, avoid feeding too many times in this age group of dogs. Around three months to six months of age, the puppy will be teething. Hence, restrict the feeding to two times only but the balanced type of nutrition needs to be provided to the dogs of this age group to avoid the deficiency based symptoms in them.

From six months to one year, try using puppy food that is available commercially. However, from first year onwards, the adult food may be given gradually. However, when the dog becomes an elder dog, restrict the frequency of feeding since the movements of such adult dogs are highly reduced due to multiple reasons. However, the pregnant animal may be fed an extra time depending on the willingness of the animal and restrict the quantity of the food but without compromising on the quality of food.

11. Signs of Ill health

Signs of ill health are the most important signs of the health status in your dogs. For example, if the dog has continuous nasal discharge, it indicates the presence of nasal congestion and if the discharge is thick, most of the times, the dog may have pneumonia.

If the dog vomits one or two times occasionally, this may not be taken as a serious sign of ill health but if the dog continues this vomiting, then this is something significant to be looked into.

If the dog has continuous itching, then one needs to check up the dog first by closer observation and examination of skin by separating the hair material especially in case of long haired breeds. You may also come across a lot of ticks or lice on skin, which may look apparently normal at a distance.

If the dog passes loose stool for one or two times, this need not be given more emphasis but if there is continuous passing of loose stool, then the dog is understood to suffer from bowel disorders. If the dog does not pass stool for two to three days, the digestive upsets needs to be ruled out carefully.

Just patiently observe the dog's walking movements and rule out any abnormal movements in the dog. If the dog is limping, the animal may have foot lesions. Similarly, if the aged dog has reluctant walking and less feed intake along with repeated vomiting, then acute renal disorders like nephritis needs to be ruled out.

If there is whiteness in eyes, suspect the corneal opacity that may occur in diseases like trypanasomosis. When the dog becomes anemic, the mucous membrane of the eyes becomes paler and in severe cases, this may have wall white color. If the dog bites chain and owners or others, look for behavior disorders and rabies needs to be ruled out.

12. Heart worm, fleas and other parasites

Heart worm, fleas and other parasites in dogs need to be eliminated by following appropriate medications in them. Many products have come up in the commercial fields to protect the dogs from heart worms, fleas and other parasites like hook worms, whip worms, round worms, lice, ticks etc.

Among the heart worm, fleas and other parasites, the fleas produce the hyper sensitive reactions in the affected animals. Hence, the animals infested with fleas start severely scratching of body. Many times, the scratching is so severe and the skin becomes more hyperemic and dermatitis occurs in the affected areas.

Animal will not lie down or sleep comfortably due to the constant bites by the fleas. Hence, animal looks as if affected by some severe skin disease. If the animal is not properly attended for this tick bite problem, there will be often secondary bacterial invasions in these sites and there may even be a bad smell emanating from the skin areas.

Close observation of the dog is highly essential to rule out the occurrence of fleas disturbing the animal to a greater extent. Similarly, the skin of the animal needs to be tested for the presence of ticks, lice etc. For this, the hair materials need to be separated and the close observation with patience is required for the proper diagnosis.

In many incidences, if anemia is present, the blood protozoa need to be ruled out in addition to the hookworm problems. The clinical problems like anemia, loose motion, pot belly etc. might be recognized by the dog owners themselves and however, the dog needs to undergo the routine health related examination involving fecal examination, hematological examination and blood smear examination.

Many commercial products have come up in the market, which are useful to deal with all these conditions by single dose. Drugs like ivermectin are highly useful and are available in both injection and oral form in addition to the solution form that can be applied on the skin. These drugs in dogs can lead to the prophylaxis of these conditions also.

13. Heart worm prevention

Beef flavored chunks are available in addition to the beef flavored tablets or solutions that can be given orally to the dogs as a measure against the incidence of heart worms. Avoid mosquito bites by providing proper mosquito-proof shelter facilities to the dogs.

Just plan whether there is any need to go for the heart worm prevention though out the year or only in some months of the year. For example, in case of some countries, the mosquitoes may be dormant in most of the colder months.

However, in some countries, this is not a position. Many a times, medications are available for oral administration to prevent heart worms along with hookworms etc. Such oral medications need to be taken as per the instructions. However, be cautious about the occurrence of any adverse drug reactions in the dog given with such prophylactic therapy.

Adverse event reports need to be sent if you come across any sorts of adverse drug reactions in your dog during the preventive treatment.
Soft beef flavored tablets are highly preferred by the pet animals as the preventive measure against heart worms. The pet owner needs to consult a veterinarian if the dose for the prophylaxis of heart worm is missed for few months. In such occasions, the pet animal needs to undergo the heart worm test.

Heartgard, sentinel, interceptor, revolution, etc. are available in the commercial fields as drugs for the preventive measure. Avoid water stagnation around the dog shelter and the bushes around the area that facilitate mosquito breeding. This test needs to be carried out in consultation with a veterinarian who is specialized in the pet animal health care and medicine.

As a preventive measure for the heart worms, the dogs need to be tested for the evidence of these worms at an age of six months. Real beef chew able tablets are available containing medical agent like ivermectin.

14. Common questions about heart worm

The common questions about heart worm are often related to the species affected by heart worms in addition to the dogs. One should know that in addition to dogs, the cat, fox, wolf, horse, sea lion etc. are also affected. Can this be cured or not? Yes. This can be treated.

What is the drug used often for the prevention of heart worm in dogs? Ivermectin is the drug used often to have preventive actions for these heart worms. Dogs affected reveal constant coughing, panting and dullness in many occasions.

What will be the size of the worms? In the case of the females, it is about twenty-seven centimeters and in the case of males, it is about seventeen centimeters in length. Is there any vector involve in the transmission of the disease? Yes. Mosquitoes often get associated as
vectors in which the early development of larvae of heart worms occur in them.

Is the prophylaxis meant only for heart worms or others also? The prophylaxis is meant not only for the heart worms but also for the hook worms, whip worms, and round worms. What is the infective type of larvae that is associated with the transmission of these heart worms? The third stage larva that is transmitted by the mosquito bites.

This occurs through out the world. In some areas, the incidences are less in colder months in which the mosquito breeding will not be there and may be dormant during these periods. What is the name of the drug used for therapy and prevention? Ivermectin and milbemycin oxime may be used for both purposes. Ivermectin is available in injection form and oral form.

Additionally, the forms for external application are also available. The cost factor needs to be worked out for all these treatments. What is the frequency of drug used for prophylaxis? One month before the mosquito season and up to two months after the mosquito season, ivermectin or milbemycin oxime may be given once monthly for the prophylaxis. Diethylcarbamazine may be used for therapy purpose.

15. Fleas and other parasites

Fleas and other parasites need to be given always a priority by the dog owners. The common incidences of flea bite allergy in case of dogs cause worries among the dog owners. Flea bite induces allergic reactions in the concerned area bitten by the fleas. Hence, the affected area looks like hairless area and the animal starts scratching.

Fleas cause severe dermatitis in dogs with severe flea infestations. Many times, the flea bite causes allergic reactions in the dogs. In many occasions, dogs experience severe discomforts due to these allergic reactions. Medicated collars are available to treat and prevent the infestation with external parasites like ticks or fleas.

Other parasites like ticks, lice in addition to the internal parasites like hook worms, round worms, whip worms etc. cause affections in the health status of the animal. For example, if hookworm affects the animal, most of the times, the dog has anemia. The anemic signs become more prominent depending on the degree of affection by the hookworm.

Hookworm larvae can pass directly through the skin and cause problems in the affected ones. Such dogs may reveal lesions pertaining to the dermatitis in the feet region and in the skin areas. Skin rashes may be seen frequently in such cases and the affected animal passes loose stool, which is of red tinged and mixed with blood material.

If the round worms are seen in more numbers, the affected puppies reveal a potbelly condition, which is easily recognized by the dog owners themselves. Piperazine salts are given by oral route for the treatment of this problem. However, broad-spectrum anthelmintics like pyrantel pamoate, fenbendazole etc. are given to treat these conditions.

Many drugs have come in market to treat the fleas and other parasites. Nowadays, the medical agent called as ivermectin is highly preferred by many dog owners to treat the fleas and other parasites in dogs. This drug is available in injection form and oral form. Even the drug is available for the external application also.

16. Do parasites cause "Scooting"?

Parasites too cause the scooting. Scooting is a an anal sac disease. First let's understand what scooting is in detail. This is the dragging of anus with the hind limbs in an extended state. Parasites causing irritation in the anus regions lead to such type of actions in animals like dogs.

However, one should not be under the impression that it is the parasite that alone causes such scooting in case of dogs. There are many occasions in which the dog may have the scooting without any parasite based etiological agent. For example, the anal gland infections, tumors at the anus and injuries near the anal regions also may lead to such type of dragging of anus region, frequently by the affected dogs.

Flea bite allergy often causes irritation at the anus region and the animal may try to bite the anus region and the irritations due to these factors lead to the final dragging of anus region on the ground. Cestodiasis in dogs is the condition caused by tapeworms.

In such occasions, if the animal is not treated in time, the animal may be seen exhibiting the scooting activities. Tapeworm segments passed in the stool create crawling like activities near anus.

Such crawling activities of the tapeworm segments lead to severe itching at these regions. Hence, to make a relief from this type of constant irritation, the animal starts pressing the anus region on the ground first and then tries to drag it on the ground with typical extension of rear limbs.

Usually there is a packet of eggs when the fecal sample is examined by microscope. However, the flotation technique leads to breakage of these packets to burst and hence, diagnosis is difficult in such occasions. Scooting dogs need to be examined to rule out tapeworm segments, which look like rice like pieces.

These segments are white in color and turn yellow when taken from the body. Tapeworms themselves may be seen in the motion or near anus below the tail regions. Consult your veterinarian for specific cures for this.

17. Preventing dental disease

Preventing dental disease is an important feature, which is to be paid more emphasis by the dog lovers or dog owners. Dental disease is given priority in the health schedule of the dog nowadays because of the association of the dental diseases with systemic diseases in the dogs.

Antibiotics need to be given in the initial stage of teeth infection itself and if not, this may cause specific infections and the organisms may spread to the other nearby regions like the oral mucous membrane and pharyngeal region etc.

More acidic or alkaline food materials need not be given to the dogs to avoid the possible teeth damage. Antibiotics need to be given in the initial stage of teeth infection itself and if not, this may cause specific infections and the organisms may spread to the other nearby regions like the oral mucous membrane and pharyngeal region etc. More acidic or alkaline food materials need not be given to the dogs to avoid the possible teeth damage. If the dog is not given at its young age some bony material to bite on, the dog may develop some dental diseases later. The teething action often causes the animal to go for biting in an indiscriminate manner. Hence, the animal has to be given some biting materials to avoid the occurrence of dental diseases.

If there is an evidence of bleeding from the oral region, the dog needs to be examined thoroughly for any dental abnormality. Mainly the puppies or some times, the adult dogs also may have teeth injuries. They need to be attended immediately as a preventive step. If not, the animal may end up in secondary bacterial infections.

Hunting dogs need additional care associated with the dental structures and such care is needed to avoid the future dental problems in such dogs. Brushes are available to provide better dental care to dogs. However, one has to allot more time and should have patience to use such brushes in case of dogs. This may lead into further problems. Centers for disease control and prevention are trying to put up guidelines to prevent the dental diseases in dogs in many nations. However, the oral examination needs to be carried out frequently in dogs and such activities help to rule out the emerging problems pertaining to the dentine structures in the beginning itself.

18. Home dental care

Home dental care is to be given more emphasis nowadays because of the fact that the dental diseases are emerging in the case of pet animals like dogs to a greater extent. Though you are giving home dental care, if you suspect on the extension of the dental diseases, then immediately approach the veterinarian for intervention.

Try to provide bone materials without very sharp points to the dogs and they may love to chew them and then swallow the bitten products. Such activities help them to go for the development of strong teeth structures in a natural manner.

Mind that the breeds of dogs like Pekingese, etc. are more prone for the development of teeth diseases because the teeth are closely crowned in the oral cavity be to the small size of the these dogs. Hence, these dogs need to be checked up for the excessive plaque formation in the home itself.

Recreational raw beef bones are wonderful materials to keep the teeth structures of your dog clean and free from formation of plaque with build up of bacterial organisms. Teeth brushes are available for use with care in case of dogs and one has to be careful during the usage of these brushes in dogs. Teeth brushes are to be used with special kinds of pastes recommended by the veterinarians for home use in case of dogs.

Specially prepared food materials are available in the pet shops to remove the tartar and the plaque materials from the teeth structures. Dry dog food and toys that are specially made to add strength to the teeth structures are often used at home for better teeth cleaning.

The plaque materials are intermittently to be removed at home to avoid any occurrence of the periodontal diseases, which are more common among the dogs. Dental wipes are available in the pet shops and they may be used carefully in the home. This helps to remove more plaque and the tartar like materials that are loosely attached.

19. Veterinary dental treatments

Veterinary dental treatments are more important. If the dental structures are not being looked carefully, there are more chances for the development of periodontal diseases in dogs. Hence, the veterinary dental treatments need to be paid maximum importance during the life of your dogs.

There are many advanced systems that deal with dental treatments that have come up in the market. Many systems are available with built in water spray systems, double filter systems, auto clavable clips, and more.

Many veterinarians use high speed fiber optic hand pieces with push button turbines, two hand piece water jet systems, soundless water compressors and more. The diagnosis of a condition pertaining to the periodontal structure based diseases are more important before the treatment.

Periodontal diseases are graded into minimal and moderate and severe diseases. Accordingly the therapy is carried out, it is impossible to check all teeth by basic oral examination in the dog patient. Hence, general anesthesia is required before the examination of the teeth inside structures. Surgical curettage is done in case of advanced periodontal diseases using flaps and the teeth extractions are also carried out using moderate force and more care is taken to avoid the continuous bleeding.

Oral surgeries are undertaken after obtaining of the dental radio graphs in the dogs and by comparing the tissue damage with normal teeth structures. The concerned veterinarians assess the extent of damage in a systematic manner.

The periodontal diseases are controlled by administration of broad-spectrum antibiotics in an effective manner. Along with the dental surgeries, the oral treatment is done with many products that are helpful to prevent the attachment of the tartar or plaque on the teeth. However, reputable products should be used in the veterinary practice and the dog owner's satisfaction is given more priority during the veterinary dental therapy.

20. The importance of the physical examination

The importance of the physical examination need not be underestimated in case of dogs. Simple but systematic physical examination techniques may diagnose most of the disorders in dogs and hence, without physical examination of the dog, one should not resort to knowing the status of your dog's health.

Simply observe the dog with scratching. Catch the dog and simply separate the hair material from the itching site. To the surprise you may come across a big wound in the scratched site. The wound might be the main reason for the scratching of the dog at that site. However, one has to rule out the occurrence of wound by severe itching itself.

Many times, when the scratching dog is examined physically, one can come across plenty of lice infestation or tick problem in the skin and coat. The parasitic condition might not be diagnosed at all if one has not carried out the physical examination. Similarly, the dog may reveal the signs of pain when the physical examination is carried out by deep palpation technique. The dog show signs of pain when the dog is examined at the stomach or the back regions.

Even if it is possible that by pressure based palpation, one can detect the acute renal disorders in the affected dogs turn to the examined site at the region of kidney or at the back region. The dog affected by the Cystitis with severe retention of urine is often diagnosed by mere physical examination.

The filled bladder together with signs of pain during the examination at the site of urinary bladder indicates that the animal is affected by Cystitis. Auscultation of the heart in both right and left sides helps to rule out the abnormal heart sounds and the pulmonary area based auscultation reveals the respiratory system disorder like pneumonia.

21. Why are regular check-ups important?

Why are regular check-ups important? Every dog owner asks this type of question, often. If you failed to do the regular check-ups, then the dog may end up having some major diseases that you don't know about. Hence, you need to pay lot of money both to the veterinarians for consultancy and for the required drugs useful for the therapy of the clinical condition.

One may not be able to find out the very commonly occurring clinical conditions in case of their dogs because of less experience with dog diseases or dog rearing. This is why check ups are important. For example, if the dog has potbelly, the condition may not look abnormal many times. But if the dog is subjected to the regular check-up, then the veterinarian immediately finds it out and gives the appropriate therapy. If not, the animal may experience diarrhea and the dehydration.

If the dog has any signs of illness, then don't wait for the regular check-up. Instead, you need to approach the veterinarian immediately. Check ups if done in a regular manner will help to give vaccinations against canine distemper, parvovirus, corona virus, rabies virus, hepatitis virus, and more.

Booster vaccinations will be carried out in such cases without any delay in the injections and this helps to improve the immunity level of the dog against such diseases in a remarkable degree. Regular check up is the essential one with proper stools examination. Hence, the deworming may be carried out with drugs like fenbendazole, albendazole, etc.

Abnormalities like signs of pain may be ruled out during such examinations. If not, helminthiasis may affect the animal and diarrhea may occur in addition to the other types of digestive upsets and anemia. Regular examinations help to rule out the external parasitic conditions like lice or tick infestations. Dental problems are also found out during the regular check ups in reputed veterinary hospitals.

22. What happens during an examination?

This question often looks so simple but holds more meanings in that. During the examination of your dog, first you need to prepare the dog first psychologically for a better-restrained status. For this, you need to take a leash and place the dog on table by the careful delivery of suitable command.

When the dog is trying to avoid the thorough examination by the veterinarian, just try to distract the dog by simple scratching of your dog behind the ears, etc. Hence, the dog's attention is some what diverted from the examination procedures that are carried out often in a systematic manner.

However, there are obedient dogs, which will remain calm during an examination. Such dogs need to be given some patting on the shoulder or the body and praises. Perhaps, many owners may try to provide some treats that are liked so much by the concerned dogs. However, it all depends on the trainings offered to the concerned dog earlier and the effective follow up procedures by the owner for the maintenance of such reflexes during the examination.

Muzzles are required for some dogs if they behave in a different manner by objecting the examination procedures by the frequent movements of the body or trying to bite the veterinarian doing the examination of the dog. Hence, the owner needs to observe the dog closely during the examination to rule out any abnormal activity by the dog.

Restraining activities in a proper manner during the clinical examination of the dog are of highly appreciable if they are successful with the concerned dogs. Such control will be of highly helpful for the effective examination of the patient by the concerned veterinarian in the pet clinic.

If the dog gets more distracted during examination by means of restlessness, then one may even use the electronic equipments which will make some sound that are audible to the dogs' ear. Such things will be helpful in the proper distraction of the animal during the examination.

23. How often should my pet be examined?

Most of the dog owners try to find this answer in a serious manner. Whatever the schedule we have for the examination of your pet animal, if there is any abnormality noticed in your animal, without delay, you need to subject the animal for a thorough clinical examination. It can be suggested that even before the purchase of a puppy, just consult a pet animal care specialist and try to understand about the schedules to be maintained for the examination of the animal. This will help a lot in solving many health related problems in the concerned animal.

Though once in two or three months is the general schedule for the examination of the dog, as soon as the puppy is procured the dog needs to be taken to the veterinarian for a thorough examination. Hence, the health care measures related program will be obtained in time. Most of the time, the dog is to be taken to the veterinarian at fifth or sixth week of age because in this period only, the vaccinations against diseases will be systematically carried out. The period of vaccination in the first year will be continued up to the sixteenth week of age and the schedule needs to be maintained accordingly.

However, if you have the pregnant dog, the dog need not be stressed by long distance based transportation for examination purposes. Hence, consult the veterinarian by phone and try to reduce the travel for the dog. However, the veterinary advice needs to be obtained in terms of health maintenance. If the dog has met with an accident either during travel or during routine movements, the animal needs to be taken to the pet hospital immediately.

Though no disease is evident, it does not mean that the dog is healthy. There are occasions wherein the animal may look like a normal dog but may have some diseases, which can be found out during the routine health check ups. Hence, the owner has to decide on when to take the dog to the hospital depending on necessity.

24. How to administer medicine

Most of the times, the dogs are so intelligent to find out the drug mixed water or food materials offered to them by the dog owners. Hence, often it becomes a headache for the dog owners to give medicines to their dogs. To the possible extent, the animal need not be forced for taking of the drug. If the medicine is to be given by mouth, first decide whether it is better to give it along with water or food. Many times, the medicines are mixed with food materials and are kept in concealed position by proper mixing of the medicine with the food materials.

Before administering the medicine, just delay the feeding time in the particular dog. Hence, the dog may be hungry to some extent. At that time, give little quantity of normal food without medicine and the dog may eat it well without any suspicion and now provide the medicine mixed food and the dog may voluntarily eat it most of the times. If the dog resists, first restraint the dog well and open the mouth. Place the tablet behind the fang teeth and almost behind the bulb of the tongue. However, take care that the medicine what you are administering in the dog should not enter directly into the respiratory organ like lungs.

If so, the dog will experience many bouts like activities and may end up in aspiration pneumonia with severe nasal discharge and panting like activities. In puppies, just swab the medicine around the upper lip. The puppy will lick automatically the drug by tongue. Hence, the administration becomes perfect in such cases.

If the medicine is in liquid form, don't raise the head of dog too much and place medicine by a syringe. Just by using a dropper, fill the medicine in the lip pocket. The continuous rubbing at the throat side may stimulate the swallowing. Making the animal thirsty and then offering of medicine mixed water may many times help the intake of the medicine.

25. Nursing a sick dog

Nursing a sick dog is one of the vital measures that a dog owner needs to understand. Similarly, when a dog becomes sick, the dog is in need of more care and affection based activities by the dog owners. Nursing a sick animal is often considered as an art and this should not be taken as a causal measure.

Yes. You need to take extra care to the dog when it becomes sick. For example, the sick dog with high fever needs to be given only some bread pieces and bulky non-vegetarian items may be avoided. Such dogs should be kept in some calm place after medications are taken and should not be disturbed. During the nursing of the dog who has taken the drug, the animal needs coaxing and stroking by the owner. Don't raise the dog's head too much to avoid the passing of drugs given by the mouth directly into the respiratory organs like lungs. During the nursing measures, take care by giving warm fluids.

Safety is to be given more priority during the nursing activity in any dog. When the dog has severe diarrhea, the animal may start showing signs of dehydration. Hence, the nursing care for dehydration includes an addition of small doses of salt and glucose to water in a careful manner.
Similarly, the vomiting dog also needs proper nursing care. Ice cubes may be given in such cases along with egg whites to smooth the esophageal passage.

Nowadays, a non-contact based infrared thermometer has come up in the market to obtain the temperature of the animal without much stress. Place the dog in a shaded place if the temperature is so high and provide good ventilation to the suffering animal. If the animal is suffering from hypothermia, provide warm blankets to given comfort to the animal.

26. Vaccinations

Vaccinations need to be undertaken always by the pet owners and the dogs need to be vaccinated at the appropriate time. This helps to improve the resistance of the animal against some specific diseases causing frequently problems in dogs. The dogs that are orphaned due to the death of the mother have lesser protection in their immune system.
Such animals are to be particularly protected against various diseases.

Vaccination is usually started at the age of five to six weeks and prior to this age, the maternal immunity will be helping the animal to have natural disease resistance. It is always better to deworm the animal before the vaccination and this is given emphasis many times. Vaccination against the parvo virus is done at an early age because pups are often being affected by parvo viral infections. The booster dose for each vaccine needs to be given at appropriate time and this helps to build up the immune status to an appreciable manner. Vaccination is carried out in many countries against rabies disease.

Hence, vaccination against rabies is given more emphasis always. Even rabies tags are fixed on to the dog collar of most of the dogs. Rabies vaccine is given at age of thirteen to fifteen weeks of age and is repeated in fifteenth months time. However, this depends on the type of vaccine used. Once in three years, this is repeated.

In dogs that have not received colostrums or dogs at high risk areas, give measles virus vaccine and killed parvovirus vaccine before five weeks of age itself. Leptospira serovar vaccine is given at six to eight weeks of age and again at tenth to twelfth weeks and at thirteenth to sixteenth weeks.

Then annually repeat this. Bordetella and lyme disease vaccinations are only optional ones in case of dogs. Vaccinations against the canine parainfluenza, canine parvovirus, and canine adenovirus type- two is similar to the schedule maintained with leptospiral serovars.

27. Common questions about vaccinations

Common questions about vaccinations are to be understood by the dog owners, as a priority. One of the common questions is whether the dog needs to be given vaccination on the first week of age or not. The dogs need not be vaccinated within five to six weeks of age. But, if they did not receive vaccinations, then the vaccination against the parvoviral infections used to kill viral vaccines and measles disease may be given.

Another common question is whether dog is to be given bordetella disease vaccine and lyme disease vaccine. No, these vaccines are only optional. Can the parvoviral vaccine can be used in first week of life? No. This will interfere with maternal antibody levels.

Can a pregnant animal be vaccinated? Yes. Two to three weeks earlier to pregnancy activity that is expected, the pregnant animal may be vaccinated against viral diseases. This helps to provide maternal antibodies to the young one to be given birth. Is there any need to give rabies vaccine to dogs? Yes. It is a must to go for the anti rabies vaccine for dogs.

When this anti-rabies vaccine is given to the dogs, what precaution does one need to undertake in this regard? Rabies vaccine is given at age of thirteen to fifteen weeks of age and should to be repeated in fifteen months and then once in three years. It is important that the dog is given this vaccine.

However, this depends on the risk area. Is there any need for canine distemper vaccination in case of dogs? Yes. There is a specific requirement in the case of dogs for the vaccination against the canine distemper. This disease is more prevalent in most of the countries.

Is there any vaccination against leptospirosis and at what age, the dog is to be vaccinated?   This is to be given at age of at six to eight weeks of age, again at tenth to twelfth weeks, and again at thirteenth to sixteenth weeks of age.

28. Spaying and neutering

Spaying and neutering of dogs are highly wanted if you don't want to breed the dogs and however, these activities need to be carried out by qualified veterinarians specialized in pet care and management. Anesthesia is required along with due surgical procedures for carrying out the spaying and neutering.

One has to understand first the terms like spaying or neutering. Both are related to the surgical approaches of sterilization in case of females and males respectively. However, the term neutering is also related to such procedures in both sexes. Accidental pregnancies that are not wanted can be highly minimized by these procedures.

Spaying and neutering helps to prevent occurrence of pyometra, which is a common reproductive disorder-giving problem to the dog owners. In male dogs, the neutering helps to prevent the occurrence of prostate enlargement or cancer. Hence, these help to minimize the incidences of reproductive disorders in dogs.

By these spaying and neutering, the male dog's desire in search of female dog in heat is highly minimized and hence, wandering of male dog is reduced. The animal becomes calm also by these surgical remedies. Territorial behavior of these animals is also highly minimized by these in case of male dogs.

Spaying of your dog before the occurrence of first heat is the best one to avoid the incidence of breast cancer. If the dog is spayed after the first heat, the chances of occurrence of breast cancer in them is more and has been proved by research. Younger group of dogs need to be subjected to these operations to avoid complications in future.

Many veterinarians prefer the spaying and neutering of dogs only at the age of five to six years. However, these can be performed even at the age of three to five years. Postoperative care needs to be followed meticulously to avoid the occurrence of infections by microbial organisms.

29. Spaying of the Female dog

Spaying of the female dog is undertaken to control the unwanted pregnancy by crossing of some unknown or country or non-descript dogs. The spaying of the dog reduces the aggressiveness of the dog. By spaying, one can reduce the incidences of the commonly encountered reproductive diseases like pyometra.

Spaying also helps to control the population in case of stray animals and many nations are doing these operations by removing the ovaries from the female animals. Experienced veterinarians are required to do the spaying in case of female dogs and the postoperative care is to be given more emphasis. If proper control measures are not taken after the surgical operation for the removal of ovary, then the infections may start setting in and the animal may end up in development of peritonitis and then toxemia sets in, causing unwanted health problems.

Death of the dog may finally occur, if the dog is not provided an effective and proper veterinary care. A female dog that is spayed before the occurrence of first heat will have almost a zero chance of development of mammary cancer, which is more common with the dogs that are not spayed.

A female dog generally comes to heat once in eight months or so. During the heat occurrence, there is bleeding from vagina and the dog may cross with the unwanted male and the spaying activity prevents all these. In case of aged dogs, the dog may often get signs of increased thirst, anorexia, vomiting etc. that are so common with pyometra.

Pyometra means the presence of pus in the uterus. Once pyometra occurs, it involves many discomforts to the animal in addition to the cost factor involved for the therapy also. Such pyometra is totally prevented by spaying because in the case of spaying, you are removing both ovaries and the uterus.

30. Surgical neutering of the male dog

Surgical neutering of the male dog is important in helping the dog owners to control the male dog's aggressive behavior. Yes. By doing the surgical neutering, it becomes possible to control the dog's restlessness, which might have caused so much agony for the owner and hence, neutering corrects such activity to the benefit of the dog owner.
When the dog is in puppy stage, the dog may be subjected to the surgical neutering technique. Hence, the hormonal impact is highly minimized in such male dogs.

The surgical neutering of the male dog helps to prevent the incidences of prostate gland diseases. Generally, in case of male dogs, the prostate enlargement is more common. In canine patients undergone the surgical neutering, the incidences of such prostate enlargement are totally minimized.

Sometimes, the adult male dog has more difficulties during defecation. However, one has to rule out the feed borne constipation like lack of fibers etc. before resorting to the fixation of prostate enlargement as a cause for this. Constipation is mainly due to the increased size of the prostate gland. Neutering makes shrinkage of the prostate gland. In surgical neutering, the incision is placed in front of the scrotum and the testicles are removed in a surgical manner using aseptic techniques.

The wound need not be closed except the tying up of the cord after cutting of the testicle. However, in two to three days time, as a routine tissue reaction, some swelling may occur in the scrotum. However, once you administer the antibiotic that has a broader spectrum of activities, the condition gets recovered in a satisfactory condition. Septic shock may occur if the surgical site gets infected with some microbial infections and in these cases, the wound needs a thorough dressing procedure and the patient needs to be continuously monitored in a clinical environment.

Take note that local animal organizations perform the surgical neutering when the stray male dogs are captured by them.

31. Pet health insurance

Pet health insurance is highly required nowadays because of the escalating cost factors pertaining to the health maintenance in dogs and other animals. Dog owners need to find pet insurance firms that settle dues to the pet owners without much delay and in a more appropriate manner. Pet health insurance firms recently come forward to settle the dues in a proper manner after the due verification of the claim. If anything happens, dog care costs can add up without insurance.

Hence, know the approved list of your local animal care hospitals. Even have the list of veterinary experts who are specialized in dog's health care and disease management measures. Many firms cover up the cost made towards undertaking of surgeries, radiographic examinations, treatment of specific conditions, laboratory fees towards undertaking of various laboratory examinations, and more. There is a weighting period before the approval of your policy by most of the insurance firms after the enrolling from you so it's good to start early.

If you don't like the insurance firm, at any time, you can cancel the insurance policy. A licensed veterinarian list should be available with all insurance firms. Many payment options are available for the pet owners.

It is better to enroll the dogs or other pets before they become adults. The animals when they are young need to be enrolled as a priority.
It is always better to the consumers who are the dog owners. Before the dogs have any illness, accidents, or get into the pre-existing conditions as quoted by many pet health insurance firms, insurance coverage needs to be entered by the dog owners. The medical history of your dog will be subjected to the full review by the insurance firms, so start soon.

32. Clipping a dog

Many dog owners generally think of clipping as only a mechanical activity. Few understand that clipping a dog is an art. Clipping a coat or nail needs to be carried out in a careful manner to avoid the injuries to the skin or nail. Clipping of the coat is to be taken care of as per the breed characteristics. If the coat is not properly clipped, this may lead to the dust accumulation in the coat and the animal may start showing signs of skin diseases. This is true especially when the grooming activities are not done in a proper manner.

Clipping of coat helps to get rid of the parasitic burden to a greater extent and also, the clipping of your dog is of more useful to expose on the type of parasitic problem that the dog is likely to suffer. Many pet health parlors are available wherein the clipping of dog will be carried out in a more systematic manner.

Always make use of a sharp clipper and in the winter regions, avoid the close clipping. This is due to the fact that the closer clipping in the winter seasons may expose the dog to the environmental stresses like the cold climate. Hence, the dog may become more vulnerable to the frostbite. Avoid the close clipping of coat or nail because this may cause injury to the underlying tissues and may cause bleeding in the concerned animal.

Many pet owners need to avoid any clipping activity when the animal is not in healthy status. Clipping instruments are available to a greater extent in many pet shops. Avoid the blunt instruments because they may not clip well and hence, repetition is required often. Always use modern equipments for clipping activities.

33. First steps in grooming

Grooming is one of the important activities to be known well by the dog owner. If the dog owner is not aware of the grooming, then the dog may encounter many types of diseases. First steps of grooming consists of activities like maintenance of coat, nails and ears. The maintenance of the coat mainly consists of enrichment measures like proper bathing, combing, drying of skin by dryers, and more. The animal need not be bathed daily and this helps to protect the skin's characteristics like insulation feature.

Use conditioners and shampoos that are meant for dogs. Combing needs to be carried out with a soft brush meant for use in case of dogs. There are varieties of brushes available and depending on the type of breeds, one can use the concerned brush. This grooming of the coat by a comb needs to be carried out daily and the fallen hair if any needs to be placed in dust bin always.

Otherwise, when the dog owners switch on the fan, the hair will fly and may enter the nostrils of persons. Always don't clip too much because this may lead to injuries of nail always. Similarly, you need to carry all the materials required for the clipping with you before the start of the procedure.

Use a sharp clipper designed for use in case of dogs. It is better to have the dog on the raised place and hence, the control of the animal is easier. Ear canals are to be checked up frequently and sterile cotton may be used for cleaning purposes. Grooming associated guidelines need to be followed strictly by the dog owners.

Nail-maintenance is one of the first steps of grooming activities. Live nail areas can be easily clipped away and are always light colored than the reddish area of the nail in the higher position. During the holding of your dog's feet by you, always have a firm grip. If not, the dog will take an upper hand during the clipping and some injury may occur.

34. Bathing a dog

Bathing a dog needs to be given more emphasis. This is because of the fact that if you are careless in bathing, the animal may end up having some infections. For example, if you don't close the ears with large cotton ball, the water may enter into ear canals and may cause some ear infections with signs like constant discharge from the ears and shaking of head.

Frequency of bathing actually depends on the breed of the dog. If the dog is of a hairy type like the cocker spaniel, then the bathing is to be carried out once in six to eight weeks. If these breeds are bathed too frequently, then the skin and coat loose the protective characters. However, when the dog has defecated on the skin due to the frequent digestive upsets leading to diarrhea, to avoid the bad smell, the dog may be subjected to frequent bathing some times by the owners.

Take more care in avoiding some irritant soaps or human soaps. The soap materials used for human beings are not suitable for dogs. Similarly, many human shampoo products are having some ingredients that are not suitable in the proportions that are to be used in case of dogs. Hence, always try to use the shampoo products that are mentioned mainly for use in dogs. Take more care in using any new product.

Always have good time and patience for products required for bathing in one place with availability of water source. Dogs love the sprinkling of water, river, and oceans. Even when you are using bathtub, have everything in one place and then start bathing of the dog. Try to have a leash, conditioner, towel, and shampoo in the bath place.

Conditioner is of helpful to make the combing activity easier later. Bathing should be a convenient activity to both the dog and the owner. This should not be a burden.

35. Pet Identification

Pet identification is highly required in these days because of the need for the licensing of the dog in a proper manner and to reduce the numbers of the stray dog menace in streets. Pet identification is done by many methods, which are different from each other. The cost factor for that also has variations accordingly.

The identification of your pet may be done by personalized tags, some times by the municipal license tag, rabies tag, and more. Most of the time, your telephone number and your name will be on a place in the personalized tags of the dogs. If any body encounters the dog accidentally during the event of missing of the dog will become capable of reporting the facts to the concerned officials.

Plastic and metal pet identification tags are available in multiple colors and the dog owners can choose the color they want. However, many select the reflective type of dog tags along with the collars. Hence, the dogs can be identified even in darkness to a greater extent.

Nowadays, many electronic gadgets are available like microchips which are embedded into the dog. However, these kinds of electronic chips need to be implanted behind the ears and once implanted, this will reveal all the data embedded in this in the computer. A collard and tagged animal makes an indication that it is not a stray animal and this gives more security to the dog.

Traditional forms of identification of the animal like tattooing is now a day not carried in dogs. Thus tracing the missed animal will become easier for the pet owners mainly due to the identification-based dog collars.

www.ingramcontent.com/pod-product-compliance
Lightning Source LLC
LaVergne TN
LVHW012128070526
838202LV00056B/5915